I0541725

Lift Your Sword

Learning to Fight God's Way and Win

Ronald Hale

Lift Your Sword: Learning to Fight God's Way and Win

Copyright © 2025 Ronald Hale

All rights reserved. Except as permitted in the U.S. Copyright Act of 1976, no part of this publication may be reproduced, distributed, or transmitted in any form or by any means, or stored in a database or retrieval system, without the prior written permission of the publisher.

Scripture References
Unless otherwise noted, all Scripture quotations are taken from multiple translations of the Bible, including but not limited to the New International Version (NIV), New Living Translation (NLT), English Standard Version (ESV), New King James Version (NKJV), and The Message (MSG). All rights for these translations are held by their respective copyright holders.

Scripture has been used with reverence and care to honor the integrity and truth of God's Word.

ISBN: 979-8-9880626-7-7
LCCN:

10 9 8 7 6 5 4 3 2 1

Printed in the United States of America
(Paperback) First Edition: June 2025

SITE PUBLISHING
7330 Staples Mill Road #106
Richmond, VA 23228

Author Information
Ronald Hale
Website: ronhalebooks.com
Email: sitepublishingtoday@gmail.com

Contents

Foreward

It is a privilege to introduce this guide on spiritual warfare; a subject that every believer must understand in today's world. The enemy is relentless, but so is the victory we have in Jesus Christ.

This book is a clear, practical, and deeply encouraging resource for anyone ready to stand firm and fight the good fight of faith. It doesn't just explain the battle; it equips you with the weapons, authority, and strategies God provides so that you can walk in freedom and power every day.

What I appreciate most is the balance between truth and grace here. It doesn't promote fear or confusion but offers hope and confidence rooted in Scripture and personal experience. The prayers and reflections throughout will inspire your own prayer life and spiritual growth.

Whether you are a new believer or a seasoned warrior, this guide will help you deepen your understanding and walk boldly in your identity as a child of God.

I encourage you to read it with an open heart and ready spirit. Let it ignite your faith, sharpen your spiritual senses, and remind you that the battle belongs to the Lord, and He has already won.

Prepare to be equipped, empowered, and encouraged to live victoriously.

Acknowledgments

First and always, thank You, God. You never leave us hanging. You show up in our weakness, meet us in our confusion, and give strength exactly when we need it most. This book exists because of Your presence and power.

To my family and friends who kept me grounded and prayed me through every step of this project, your love means the world.

To those mentors and fellow believers who have taught me so much about faith, courage, and spiritual warfare; you inspire me every day.

And to you, the one holding this book; thank you for trusting me to walk alongside you. I pray every word strengthens your hands, sharpens your spirit, and reminds you that Jesus has already won the battle.

You're not alone. You were never meant to fight alone. We're in this together.

Introduction

Warning: You're in a War You Didn't Even Know About

There's an enemy out there, and he hates you. He's not after your money, your job, or your status. He wants something far more valuable: **your soul**.

His goal? To separate you from God, steal your joy, and keep you trapped in lies.

And the scariest part? Most people don't even realize the fight is happening.

This battle isn't fought with fists or guns. It's a **spiritual war**; a fight for your mind, your heart, and your eternal destiny. The enemy is clever, subtle, and relentless. He uses fear, shame, distraction, compromise, and confusion to keep you stuck, silent, and defeated.

But here's the powerful truth: you don't have to lose. Jesus already came, fought, and won.

He didn't just die to forgive your sins. He destroyed the power of darkness. He exposed the enemy's tactics, conquered death, and walked out of the grave holding victory in His hands. And then He gave that victory to you.

You're not just saved, you're **equipped**. You're not just rescued, you're recruited.

God has given you spiritual armor, divine authority, and the power of the Holy Spirit to stand strong and fight back.

This book is your **battle guide**. Whether you're waking up to this war for the first time or have been fighting for years, here you'll find clear, practical steps, biblical truth, and spiritual activation to help you:

- Recognize the enemy's tactics
- Break strongholds and generational patterns
- Put on the full armor of God
- Use your God-given authority
- Live in daily victory, freedom, and purpose

Most of all, you'll be reminded of who you really are; not weak, not forgotten, not a victim.

You are a child of God: chosen, covered, and equipped to fight and win.

This is your moment to wake up, rise up, and step fully into the power Jesus already won for you.

The war is real. But so is your victory.

And your training starts now.

Dedication

This book is for you; the one who's tired of feeling overwhelmed by the battles you can't see. You're not alone in this fight. Jesus is with you, and so am I.

I wrote this to remind you that you can stand strong, that victory is real, and that your life matters in this spiritual battle.

Keep going. Keep pressing in. You've got what it takes, because the One who fights for you has **never** lost a battle.

Note to the Reader

Just a Reminder Before You Dive In:

This guide was written to help you grow in spiritual strength, learn how to fight the right way, and walk in the freedom Jesus died to give you. But here's something important: don't just take my word for it.

Be like the Bereans in **Acts 17**. They didn't just listen and move on; they took what they heard and checked it against Scripture. They made sure it lined up with God's truth. You should do the same.

As you read through this guide, stay in the Word. Ask God to show you what's true, what applies to your life, and where He's leading you. Let the Bible be your final authority, not this book or any other.

This guide is a tool, but the **Word of God is your sword**. **Study it. Know it. Live it.**

"Study to show yourself approved unto God…"
—2 Timothy 2:15

Chapter 1
Known in Hell

Scripture Focus: Acts 19:13–16
"Jesus I know, and Paul I know; but who are you?" (Acts 19:15)

Imagine a group of men with impressive backgrounds; they're sons of a Jewish high priest, familiar with religious rituals and the sacred language of their faith. They believe they have what it takes to confront dark forces. Armed with the right words, they attempt to cast out demons using the name of Jesus, just like the Apostle Paul did. But suddenly, the demons turn on them with violent force, leaving them stripped, battered, and running for their lives.

Why?

Because spiritual authority doesn't come from titles or repeating words. It comes from truly knowing Jesus. It's built on relationship, obedience, and a life fully surrendered to His power.

The story of the seven sons of Sceva (**Acts 19:13–16**) is sobering. They had religious credentials and all the right spiritual language, but none of it mattered. The enemy hit them with a question that still stops people in their tracks today: **"Jesus I know, and Paul I know; but who are you?"**

What Does It Mean to Be "Known in Hell"?

The spiritual realm is real, and far more structured than we think. Scripture makes it clear: darkness isn't chaotic or clueless. It's calculated, alert, and watching. It recognizes true authority; those marked by God's presence, and it quickly exposes every counterfeit.

Think about it like this: If someone claims to be a professional basketball player but never trained, never studied the game, and doesn't even know how to dribble. Would real players take them seriously? Not a chance. They wouldn't last a minute in the league. On the court, they'd be exposed, overwhelmed, and completely outclassed.

In the same way, you can't fake authority in spiritual warfare. Hell can tell who's walking in real power, and who's just pretending.

Authority Is Not About Performance

Many people think that shouting the name of Jesus or using Christian "church talk" gives them spiritual power. **But the truth is, authority flows from your relationship with God, not performance.**

- Paul didn't just repeat Jesus' name, he knew Jesus personally.
- He lived a surrendered life, marked by obedience and power.
- Hell feared Paul because his life backed up his words.

Authority comes from proximity to Jesus, not just a loud voice or impressive religious credentials. You cannot borrow authority from others or fake it. It is granted by intimacy with God and faithfulness in daily living.

Real-Life Example: Elijah on Mount Carmel

Let's look at Elijah in **1 Kings 18**. He faced the prophets of Baal, a powerful religious group with many followers. Elijah didn't just talk loudly or make empty claims. He prayed with authority because he had a history with God. His obedience and trust made his prayers effective, and heaven answered with fire.

Elijah's story shows that true spiritual authority is recognized by heaven and feared by hell because it is rooted in genuine faith and obedience.

What Happens When You Don't Have Real Authority?

Going back to the sons of Sceva, they tried to imitate Paul by using his words without living his life. They said, "In the name of Jesus, whom Paul preaches," but the spiritual forces of darkness they faced didn't know who they were.

The enemy mocked them and overpowered them. The lesson? **Words alone do not have power; they must be matched by a life surrendered to God.**

Many people today are like the sons of Sceva. They use Christian language, attend church, maybe even serve in ministry, but they don't actually know Jesus in a personal, life-changing way. That's a dangerous place to be. Why? Because the enemy isn't threatened by religious words or surface-level faith. He's looking for people who are spiritually unprotected; those who are disconnected from God or careless with their choices.

When we live like that, we leave cracks in the door of our hearts, and the enemy doesn't hesitate to slip through. He enters through things like bitterness, compromise, unforgiveness, or secret sin. Once inside, he begins to influence our thinking, stir up confusion, and weigh us down with fear, guilt, or shame.

That's what the Bible means by **bondage**; when something begins to control or limit you in ways you can't seem to break free from. But here's the good news: when you truly know Jesus and walk closely with Him, the enemy loses his grip. You don't have to live bound. You can live free.

Why Does This Matter for You?

Whether you're new to faith or have walked with God for years, this chapter is a wake-up call: **Is your spiritual life real or just routine?**

Do you truly know Jesus, or are you coasting on borrowed phrases and secondhand faith?

You might go to church, say the right things, and even read your Bible, but does your life reflect His power, His presence, and His authority?

Because here's the truth:

1. The enemy isn't intimidated by religion.
2. He doesn't flinch at church attendance or spiritual talk.
3. He recognizes, and fears those who actually walk with God.

When your life is marked by obedience, intimacy, and faith, **hell takes notice.**

You become known in hell, not because of who you are, but because of **Who walks with you.**

Reflection Questions:

- Am I walking in borrowed faith or genuine relationship with Jesus?
- Does my life show evidence of God's power, or am I just repeating words?

- When I face spiritual battles, do I rely on Jesus or my own strength?
- Where is God inviting me to grow deeper in intimacy, trust, and daily obedience?

Activation Prayer: "Make Me Known in Heaven, and Feared in Hell"

Father,

I don't want to pretend or fake my faith. I want to know You deeply, not just say Your name. Train me in intimacy with You. Let my life be marked by obedience, not just words. Make me unshakable because I walk with You every day. Let my prayers shake the gates of hell, not because of who I am, but because of who You are in me. Jesus, make me dangerous to darkness.

In Your mighty name,

Amen.

Testimony Prompt:

Think of a time when you tried to face a spiritual challenge or fear without fully trusting God. What happened? What did you learn about relying on Jesus versus relying on your own strength or knowledge?

Action Step:

This week, set aside quiet time to pray and ask God to reveal areas where your faith is shallow or disconnected. Invite Him to deepen your relationship and strengthen your spiritual authority.

Final Thought

Your spiritual authority is not about impressing others or sounding spiritual; it's about being known by God and feared by the enemy. Hell knows who walks with Jesus. Will your life be one of true power, or just borrowed words?

Chapter 2

The Power of Jesus' Name

Scripture Focus: Philippians 2:9-11

"Therefore God exalted him to the highest place and gave him the name that is above every name, that at the name of Jesus every knee should bow, in heaven and on earth and under the earth…"

You've probably heard people say, "There's power in the name of Jesus." Maybe you've even said it yourself. But what does that really mean? How does simply saying His name carry power? And what difference does it make in your everyday life, especially when facing challenges or spiritual battles?

Let's unpack this together. Because understanding the power of Jesus' name isn't just about memorizing a phrase, it's about living in the reality of who Jesus is and what His name represents.

Why Is the Name of Jesus So Powerful?

The Bible tells us that God exalted Jesus to the highest place and gave Him a name above every other name. That's a big deal.

Think about names in your life. Names identify, represent, and hold meaning. When someone calls your name, it grabs your attention because it's connected to your identity. Now, Jesus' name isn't just a label, it carries authority and power over everything in heaven, earth, and even the spiritual realm.

There's a story in **Acts 3** that shows this power in action. Peter and John were walking when they saw a man who had been lame from birth begging at the temple gate. Peter said, "In the name of Jesus Christ of Nazareth, walk." And right there, the man stood up and walked! Not because of Peter's power, but because of the power in Jesus' name.

What Does It Mean to Use Jesus' Name?

Using Jesus' name isn't about repeating a special phrase or treating it like a spiritual formula. It's not about saying the right words in the right order. It means standing in His authority, knowing who He is, and believing in the power behind His name.

In **John 14:13**, Jesus said, "And I will do whatever you ask in my name, so that the Father may be glorified in the Son." That means when you act in Jesus' name, you're not just speaking; it's an act of faith and alignment with His will. His name represents His presence, His victory, and His authority over every power of darkness.

His name isn't something we just say; it's something we live under and walk in.

Real-Life Example: The Name in Action

There's a powerful story of a woman named Mary (name changed for privacy) who was trapped in addiction for years. She tried everything, counseling, willpower, support groups; but nothing could break the chains.

One day, a friend prayed over her, boldly speaking the name of Jesus. Mary told me later that in that moment, something shifted inside her; a peace she had never felt before. Over time, she experienced freedom that no human effort could give.

This is the power of Jesus' name at work; breaking chains, healing wounds, and bringing life where there was death.

What Happens When You Use Jesus' Name in Spiritual Warfare?

When the Bible talks about spiritual warfare, Jesus' name is the key weapon. Demons recognize the authority behind His name. That's why Paul and the disciples used it when they cast out evil spirits.

Remember the story from chapter 1 about the sons of Sceva? They tried to use Jesus' name without truly knowing Him, and it backfired. The difference was relationship and authority, not just words.

How Can You Start Using the Power of Jesus' Name?

- **Know Who Jesus Is**
  Don't just say His name, know His character, His love, His power. Spend time reading the Gospels to meet Jesus for yourself.

- **Believe in His Authority**
  Faith activates power. Believe that Jesus is alive, reigning, and working on your behalf.

- **Pray Boldly in His Name**
  When you pray, don't just say "in Jesus' name" as a closing line; declare it with confidence and expectation.

- **Speak Truth Over Your Life**
  Use Jesus' name to declare freedom, healing, peace, and victory over circumstances and strongholds.

Reflection: Where Do I Stand with the Name of Jesus?

- Do I understand the authority behind Jesus' name?
- Am I using His name confidently or out of habit?
- How can I deepen my relationship with Jesus to walk in His power daily?

Activation Prayer: "I Declare the Power of Jesus' Name"

Jesus,

Thank You for Your powerful name, which is above every name. Help me to know You more deeply, to understand the authority I carry when I speak Your name. Give me boldness to pray and act in Your name, trusting in Your power to bring freedom and victory. Let Your name be my refuge and strength, my weapon and my song. Use me to show Your love and power to those around me.

In Your powerful name, Jesus, I pray,

Amen.

Chapter 3
The Authority of the Believer

Scripture Focus: Luke 10:19
"I have given you authority to trample on snakes and scorpions and to overcome all the power of the enemy; nothing will harm you."

You might think, **Authority?** For me? If you grew up hearing about spiritual battles or saw ministries praying over, healing and deliverance, you might think authority is reserved for pastors, missionaries, or spiritual "superstars." But the truth is, Jesus has given **every believer authority**. Yes, you included.

The authority comes with the mission and the connection.

What Does "Authority" Mean Here?

Authority means the **right and power** to act and make decisions. Spiritually, it means God has given you the power to stand against the enemy's attacks, to speak truth, and to live in freedom.

Jesus didn't keep this power for Himself or just a select few. Right before He ascended to heaven, He told His followers: "I have given you authority…" He passed on this spiritual power to us as His followers.

Why Does This Matter?

Imagine being handed the keys to a powerful kingdom; not just to hold, but to use. Not as a guest, but as someone with full access and responsibility. These keys unlock doors, shut out intruders, and give you freedom to move with confidence and authority. That's what Jesus has done. He didn't just save you, He entrusted you with the keys to His Kingdom.

You've been given real access to His power, His promises, and His authority to stand against darkness and bring heaven to earth.

In **Matthew 16:19**, Jesus says:
"I will give you the keys of the kingdom of heaven; whatever you bind on earth will be bound in heaven, and whatever you loose on earth will be loosed in heaven."

Let's make that simple.

To **bind** something means to forbid it, shut it down, or tell it, "You have no place here."
To **loose** something means to release it, welcome it, or allow it to flow freely.

This isn't about formulas. It's about **authority**.

- You can **bind** fear, confusion, or oppression when it tries to take hold of your mind or your home.
- You can **loose** peace, healing, clarity, and truth; everything that reflects God's heart.

Jesus is saying, **"Here are the keys. Use them."**

This is the kind of authority He's trusted you with; not to control people, but to align your life and circumstances with

Heaven's will. You don't have to put up with everything that knocks on your door. Through prayer, you can spiritually stand at the door and say, *"This stays. That goes."*

The Reality Check: Authority vs. Power

It's important to understand there's a difference between authority and power. Power is raw energy; without direction it can be chaotic or even destructive. Authority is power used with responsibility, wisdom, and purpose.

God's authority given to you is always exercised in alignment with His will and character. It's not about controlling others or acting in pride. It's about standing firm in truth and love.

Real-Life Example: Taking Authority at Work

Using Jesus' name isn't just for dramatic moments of spiritual warfare; it applies to your everyday environment, too.

Joshua works in an office where tension always seems to run high. People gossip behind each other's backs, there's constant miscommunication, and the atmosphere feels toxic and discouraging. Even though he's doing his job well, he goes home drained, like something more than just "work stress" is weighing on him.

One morning before anyone else arrives, Joshua decides to pray. Not just a quiet prayer under his breath, but a bold declaration in Jesus' name; spoken softly, but with real authority.

He walks through the office slowly and says:

> "In Jesus' name, I bind every spirit of confusion, division, and discouragement that's been trying to dominate this place. You have no authority here."

Then he continues:

> "I loose God's peace, clarity, and unity over this office. I speak favor, integrity, and cooperation into this environment. Let this be a place where people work with joy and respect."

He doesn't make a scene. He just takes a few quiet moments to speak truth and shift the spiritual atmosphere.

Over the next week, Joshua starts noticing changes. A co-worker who's usually bitter starts opening up. Team meetings go more smoothly. Even the manager, who's been distant and cold, seems a little warmer.

Did Joshua fix everything overnight? No. But something shifted. That's how spiritual authority works. It doesn't always shout, but it does stand firm. He wasn't powerless. He was partnered with Jesus, using the keys of the kingdom right where he was planted.

This is the kind of authority available to every believer; not to dominate people, but to partner with God in inviting His will into real spaces.

How to Walk in Your Authority Daily

- **Know Your Position**
  Remember, you're seated with Christ in heavenly places (Ephesians 2:6). This means you share in His authority.
- **Use Your Authority with Faith**
  Speak boldly, knowing you represent Jesus. Don't shrink back, but don't try to control outcomes; trust God's timing.
- **Submit to God's Will**
  Authority flows from obedience and humility. God's authority isn't about self-will but partnership with His Spirit.
- **Stand Firm**
  You will face opposition, but don't retreat. Jesus promised victory over the enemy.

What About When We Feel Weak?

Feeling powerless sometimes is normal. Remember, authority doesn't come from your feelings but from God's promises and Jesus' victory. Faith grows when we choose to trust God even when we don't feel strong.

Reflection: Am I Living in My Authority?

- Do I believe I have authority because Jesus gave it to me?
- How often do I speak or act with that authority?
- Where do I struggle to stand firm against the enemy?
- Am I submitting my will to God while using this authority?

Activation Prayer: "Help Me Walk in Authority"

Lord Jesus,

Thank You for giving me authority over the enemy's schemes. Teach me to walk boldly in this authority every day, not out of pride, but out of obedience to You. Help me to recognize the power You have given me and to use it with wisdom and humility. Strengthen my faith when I feel weak, and remind me that victory is already mine through You.

In Your mighty name,

Amen.

Chapter 4
The Role of the Holy Spirit in Warfare

Scripture Focus: John 14:26
"But the Advocate, the Holy Spirit, whom the Father will send in my name, will teach you all things and will remind you of everything I have said to you."

If spiritual warfare is a battle, then the Holy Spirit is your trusted guide, strategist, and power source. You're not left to fight alone or with your own strength; God's Spirit lives inside you to lead, empower, and protect.

Who Is the Holy Spirit?

Think of the Holy Spirit as God's presence and power available to live inside believers. Jesus called Him the Advocate, the Helper, the Comforter, someone who stands with you, speaks truth, and helps you navigate the unseen spiritual world.

When it comes to warfare, the Spirit doesn't just give you power to fight; He gives you wisdom, discernment, and peace.

Why You Need the Holy Spirit in Battle

Imagine stepping onto a battlefield blindfolded; swinging at shadows, unsure where the real threat is coming from. That's what it's like trying to fight spiritual battles without the Holy Spirit. The enemy doesn't play fair. He hides in confusion, cloaks his attacks in half-truths, and lays traps beneath what looks like normal life.

But the Holy Spirit is your divine Counselor, your supernatural Guide, your front-line Intel. He's not just your GPS, He's your war strategist. He reveals the unseen, exposes deception, and gives you divine insight before the enemy strikes.

Without Him, you'll fight in the flesh and wear yourself out. But with Him, you fight from victory, not for it. He gives you discernment to see beyond the surface, courage when fear creeps in, and wisdom that no man can give. He'll prompt you when to speak and when to stay silent, when to stand still and when to move in power.

He's the whisper behind your obedience, the fire in your prayers, and the power that turns ordinary believers into spiritual warriors.

This is more than just comfort; it's survival. In these days, deception is growing, and compromise is subtle. You need more than head knowledge; you need revelation. **You need the Holy Spirit**.

Real-Life Story: Hearing the Spirit's Voice: Bruce's Battle

Bruce was a father, a husband, and a leader in his local church. On the outside, everything looked good. But inside, he was silently drowning in spiritual confusion. Thoughts of failure haunted him: "You're not enough." "You've already messed it up." "God can't use someone like you."

At first, Bruce thought these were just internal insecurities, but over time, the burden grew heavier. He began waking up in the middle of the night with dread, feeling distracted during prayer, and numb in worship. His mind felt like a war zone, and nothing he did seemed to bring relief.

One evening, after another restless night, Bruce finally sat still before God; not with noise or long prayers, but in quiet surrender. In the silence, something shifted. In the middle of all the noise in his mind, a clear and gentle voice rose like peace breaking through confusion: "That's not Me speaking."

It startled him.

The thought came again, like a soft light breaking through the darkness.

"The voice accusing you? That's not My voice. My sheep know My voice. I lead through peace, not shame."

Bruce broke down. Tears streamed down his face; not from guilt, but from the relief of finally hearing the truth. He realized he had been listening to the enemy's voice wrapped in religious language. Guilt pretending to be God. Lies disguised as honest self-reflection.

From that day forward, Bruce began to test the voices in his mind. He learned to recognize the enemy's attacks versus the Spirit's guidance.

- The Holy Spirit's voice brought clarity, not confusion.
- Hope, not fear.
- Correction, yes, but always with the kindness that leads to repentance.
- Peace, even when the truth cut deep.

Bruce didn't become perfect overnight, but he became free. He learned to pause, ask, and listen. He learned to listen closely to the Spirit by practicing patience, staying humble, and quieting his heart. As he did, the enemy's lies began to lose their hold.

Practical Insight: How to Recognize the Spirit's Voice

Many believers struggle like Bruce; not because God isn't speaking, but because they haven't learned to recognize His voice amid the noise. Here are a few questions to help:

- **Does this voice align with Scripture?**
  The Holy Spirit will never contradict God's Word.
- **Does it produce peace or fear?**
  The Spirit may convict, but He never condemns. His correction carries peace.
- **Is this voice leading me toward freedom or keeping me in shame?**
  The enemy accuses. The Spirit invites.
- **Is this urgent and chaotic, or steady and firm?**
  The devil rushes. The Spirit leads.

When you learn to discern the Spirit's voice, you don't just win a moment, you gain a lifelong weapon in spiritual warfare.

The Holy Spirit Gives You These in Warfare:

- **Wisdom:** To know when and how to pray, speak, or act (James 1:5).
- **Discernment:** To recognize enemy tactics and spiritual attacks (1 Corinthians 2:14).
- **Boldness:** To confront darkness without fear (Acts 4:31).
- **Power:** To heal, deliver, and resist temptation (Acts 1:8).
- **Peace:** To stand firm when storms come (Philippians 4:7).

How to Partner with the Holy Spirit Daily

- **Stay Connected Through Prayer**
  Ask the Spirit to guide your thoughts, words, and actions.
- **Read and Meditate on God's Word**
  The Spirit will bring Scriptures to mind that help you in battle.

- **Practice Obedience**
  When the Spirit prompts you, respond quickly; even if it feels uncomfortable.
- **Invite the Spirit's Presence**
  Before facing challenges, pray for His power and protection.
- **Cultivate Sensitivity**
  Quiet your heart to hear the Spirit's voice. He won't shout but gently leads.

What Happens If You Ignore the Spirit?

Trying to fight spiritual battles without the Holy Spirit is like trying to win a war with no strategy or weapons. You'll feel powerless, confused, or defeated. The Spirit empowers us to be more than conquerors (Romans 8:37).

Reflection: Am I Walking with the Spirit in My Battles?

- Do I regularly ask the Holy Spirit for help in my spiritual struggles?
- Can I recognize when He is speaking or guiding me?
- How willing am I to obey His promptings even when it's hard?
- Am I relying on my own strength or His power?

Activation Prayer: "Fill Me with Your Spirit"

Holy Spirit,

I invite You to fill me anew. Teach me to hear Your voice clearly and follow Your lead. Give me wisdom to recognize the enemy's schemes and courage to stand firm. Empower me with Your strength, boldness, and peace as I walk through spiritual battles. Help me not to rely on my own power, but to lean fully on You. Thank You for being my Guide and Helper every day.

In Jesus' name,

Amen.

Chapter 5
Spiritual Armor Explained

Scripture Focus: Ephesians 6:10-18
"Put on the full armor of God, so that you can take your stand against the devil's schemes."

If you're new to spiritual warfare, the idea of "putting on armor" might sound strange or even a bit old-fashioned. But this armor isn't about metal helmets or shields; it's about real protection in a real battle that's happening all around and within us.

Paul's letter to the Ephesians gives us a powerful picture of what God's armor looks like and how it helps us stand firm when the enemy attacks.

Why Armor?

Think about a soldier getting ready for battle. They wouldn't show up wearing Jordans and a t-shirt, right? They gear up with the right equipment to protect their body and give them strength. In the same way, God equips you with spiritual gear to protect your heart, mind, and soul.

The enemy wants to weaken you, steal your peace, and steal your destiny. But with God's armor, you're ready to resist and stand victorious.

The Pieces of God's Armor

Let's break down what each piece means, so you can not only know them but start using them daily.

1. The Belt of Truth

The belt holds everything together for a soldier. Without it, the armor falls apart. Truth does the same in your life. When you know who you are in Christ and what God says about you, you're grounded and unshakable. Lies from the enemy lose their power when you stand on God's truth.

Example: When fear whispers "You're worthless," truth says, "I am God's beloved child."

2. The Breastplate of Righteousness

This protects the heart and vital organs. Righteousness means living in right standing with God, not because you're perfect, but because of Jesus' work on your behalf. It guards your heart against guilt, condemnation, and shame: some of the enemy's favorite weapons.

3. The Shoes of the Gospel of Peace

Imagine walking into a chaotic place but having peace underneath your feet. The gospel. The good news of Jesus gives you confidence and readiness to move forward even when battles come. Peace keeps you steady.

4. The Shield of Faith

The shield blocks fiery arrows; attacks from the enemy designed to cause doubt and fear. Faith is your defense. When you trust God's promises even when things look impossible, you stop the enemy's attacks in their tracks.

5. The Helmet of Salvation

The helmet protects the mind. Salvation means your mind is guarded because you know your eternal future is secure in Christ. This protection helps you reject thoughts of defeat, despair, or worthlessness.

6. The Sword of the Spirit (God's Word)

This is the only offensive weapon in the armor. God's Word is powerful; it pierces lies, breaks chains, and brings freedom. Jesus used Scripture to resist Satan's temptations. The Bible is your weapon for every battle.

Real-Life Story: Using the Armor Daily

Mark didn't realize how distracted he was until the distractions stopped helping. He filled his time with music, TV, and scrolling through social media, but deep down, he felt empty. Negative thoughts kept showing up: "You're not good enough." "Why bother?"

One day, it hit him; he'd been using noise to cover up what was really going on. He felt spiritually unprotected, like walking into battle with no armor on.

So he made a change. Every morning, Mark started "putting on" God's armor. He'd whisper truth and life over himself while getting ready:
"I have the belt of truth. I know who I am in Christ."
"I hold up the shield of faith. I trust God today."

When lies tried to sneak in, he'd speak Scripture out loud and remind himself of what God says.

Over time, those daily choices rewired how Mark saw spiritual battle; not as something to fear, but something to face with power, dressed and ready.

How to Put On the Armor

- Start your day intentionally: Pray through each piece, asking God to clothe you.
- Meditate on the meaning of each piece and how it applies to your life.
- Use Scripture as your sword. Know key verses to combat lies or fear.
- Be alert throughout your day; watch for enemy attacks and respond with your armor.
- Remember, the armor is spiritual. It works best when you walk in relationship with God.

What Happens Without the Armor?

Without God's armor, you're wide open to attack. The enemy looks for weak spots, like a mind full of worry, a heart heavy with guilt, or faith that's barely hanging on. That's when life starts to feel too hard, and giving up feels easier than fighting.

But here's the good news: you don't have to be perfect or have it all together. God's armor is ready whenever you are. The moment you choose to put it on, you're covered and protected.

Reflection: Am I Dressed for Battle?

- Do I understand the armor God offers?
- How often do I consciously "put on" this armor in my daily routine?
- Which piece do I need to strengthen or focus on more?
- Am I ready to stand firm and resist the enemy today?

Activation Prayer: "Clothe Me in Your Armor"

Father God,

Thank You for the armor You give me to stand strong in the spiritual battle. Help me to put on Your truth, righteousness, peace, faith, salvation, and Your powerful Word every day. When the enemy attacks, remind me I am protected and victorious in You. Give me the strength to stand firm and the courage to fight from a place of power, not fear. Clothe me fully in Your armor, and help me walk boldly as Your warrior.

In Jesus' name,

Amen.

Chapter 6
The Battlefield of the Mind

Scripture Focus: 2 Corinthians 10:3-5
"For though we live in the world, we do not wage war as the world does. The weapons we fight with are not the weapons of the world. On the contrary, they have divine power to demolish strongholds. We demolish arguments and every pretension that sets itself up against the knowledge of God, and we take captive every thought to make it obedient to Christ."

Welcome to the front line: the battlefield of your mind.

If you think spiritual warfare is mostly about external attacks, demonic oppression, difficult people, or bad circumstances, you're only seeing part of the picture. The most intense battles happen inside, in the hidden places where thoughts, doubts, and emotions collide.

The mind is ground zero for spiritual warfare. Why? Because what you think influences how you feel, what you say, and what you do. The enemy knows this and relentlessly targets your thoughts.

Why the Mind Matters

Imagine trying to run a race with a 25-pound barbell on your shoulders. That's what it's like when your mind is weighed down with fear, lies, anxiety, or confusion. You're exhausted before you even start, and you can't run freely like that.

God wants your mind free and renewed. **Romans 12:2** tells us, "Do not conform to the pattern of this world, but be transformed by the renewing of your mind." The enemy's goal is to keep your mind stuck in old patterns that pull you away from God's truth and freedom.

The Enemy's Strategies in the Mind

1. Lies and Deception
The devil is called the father of lies for a reason (**John 8:44**). He fills your mind with falsehoods: "You're not good enough," "God doesn't love you," "You'll never change." Lies are designed to confuse and discourage.

2. Fear and Anxiety
Fear says, "You can't handle this." Anxiety says, "What if everything goes wrong?" Both are meant to paralyze you, to keep you stuck and inactive.

3. Doubt and Confusion
Doubt questions God's promises and your identity. Confusion clouds your ability to hear God's voice or know what step to take next.

4. Negative Thought Cycles
The enemy loves to trap you in repeating negative thoughts, like a broken record: "I always fail," "I'm alone," "Nothing will ever get better."

How God Wants You to Fight

The good news is you don't have to let these attacks win. God gives you weapons to fight back, and they have divine power.

Paul's words in **2 Corinthians 10:5** are key: "*We take captive every thought to make it obedient to Christ*." Capturing thoughts means you don't let every idea or feeling control you. You decide which ones stay and which ones go.

Practical Steps to Win Your Mind's Battles

1. Identify the Lies
Start by listening to your thoughts. What is the enemy saying to you? Write down any negative or fearful thoughts. When you see them clearly, it's easier to challenge them.

2. Replace Lies with Truth
Once you identify a lie, counter it with God's truth. For example, if the enemy says, "You're worthless," replace it with, "I am fearfully and wonderfully made" (**Psalm 139:14**). Write down Scripture verses that speak truth over your life.

3. Pray and Declare God's Word
Prayer is your frontline defense. Speak God's promises out loud. For example: "I have not been given a spirit of fear, but of power, love, and a sound mind" (**2 Timothy 1:7**). Declare freedom over your thoughts.

4. Meditate on Scripture
Choose a verse or passage to focus on each day. Let it fill your mind. Meditation renews your thinking and draws you closer to God.

5. Take Every Thought Captive
When a negative thought comes, stop it. Say, 'No, this thought is not from God.' Don't let it linger. Refuse to entertain it. Replace it with a prayer, a Bible verse, or a simple reminder of God's truth. The sooner you respond, the less power the lie has to shape your mindset, your mood, or your decisions.

Real-Life Story: Hannah's Journey to Peace
(Hannah's story is from 1 Samuel 1)

Hannah was very sad because she couldn't have a child. Her mind was full of worry and sadness, but she chose not to let those thoughts control her. Instead, she went to God and honestly shared how she felt, asking Him for help.

Even though it was hard, Hannah trusted God's plan and didn't give in to fear or doubt. She prayed with faith, believing God was listening. Because she kept trusting God, He gave her a son, just as He promised.

Hannah's story shows us that when we don't let our worries rule us and instead put our trust in God, He can bring hope and blessings; even when things seem impossible.

Common Questions and Misconceptions

"Does that mean I'll never have negative thoughts?"
No. Everyone has unwanted thoughts sometimes. The difference is what you do with them. You have the choice to reject or accept them.

"Is this just positive thinking?"
No. Spiritual warfare in the mind is more than just staying positive. It's about aligning your thoughts with God's Word, even when circumstances are hard.

"What if I don't know Scripture well?"
Start simple. Memorize a few key verses that encourage you. Then, ask God to help you understand and apply His Word, because as **James 1:5** reminds us, God gives wisdom generously to everyone who asks without finding fault.

Reflection: What's Going on in Your Mind?

- What are the most common thoughts you have about yourself?
- Are those thoughts true or lies?
- How do those thoughts affect your emotions and actions?
- What Scripture can you use to replace negative thoughts?
- Are you ready to take every thought captive and make it obedient to Christ?

Activation Prayer: "Renew My Mind, Lord"

Father,

I bring my mind before You today. I confess that sometimes my thoughts are tangled with fear, lies, and confusion. Please forgive me for allowing these to have power over me. Renew my mind with Your truth. Help me recognize the enemy's lies and replace them with Your Word. Teach me to take every thought captive and make it obedient to You. Fill me with Your peace that surpasses all understanding. Strengthen me to walk in the freedom You have already won.

In Jesus' name,

Amen.

Action Step: Mind Battle Journal

Start a journal specifically for your mind battles. Each day, write down:
- Negative thoughts or lies you noticed
- The Scripture you used to counter them
- How you felt afterward
- Any breakthrough or progress you experienced

This practice trains your mind and builds your faith muscle.

Final Encouragement

The battlefield of the mind can feel overwhelming, but remember: you're not alone, and you're not powerless. God's Spirit lives in you, giving you wisdom, strength, and victory. The moment you start capturing your thoughts and aligning them with God's truth, you're stepping into freedom.

Keep pressing in, keep renewing, and keep standing firm. Your mind is one of your greatest battlegrounds, and with God's help, it can also be one of your greatest victories.

Chapter 7
Prayer Strategies in Warfare

Scripture Focus: Ephesians 6:18

"And pray in the Spirit on all occasions with all kinds of prayers and requests. With this in mind, be alert and always keep on praying for all the Lord's people."

Let's talk about prayer. It's one of your strongest weapons in spiritual battle.

Prayer is not just a spiritual activity; it's your lifeline and your offensive weapon in the battle. But prayer isn't always easy. Sometimes it feels like talking to an empty room, or like your prayers bounce off the ceiling without any impact.

This chapter will guide you through powerful prayer strategies designed for spiritual warfare; helping you pray boldly, effectively, and in alignment with God's will.

Why Prayer Is One Of Your Most Powerful Weapons

Before diving into strategies, it's important to understand why prayer is so crucial in spiritual warfare:

- **Prayer connects you to God's authority.** The battle isn't fought with your strength but God's power flowing through you.

- **Prayer shifts the spiritual atmosphere.** It can break strongholds, silence the enemy's plans, and release heaven's intervention.

- **Prayer keeps you alert and spiritually sensitive.** It helps you discern the enemy's tactics and respond wisely.

- **Prayer activates your faith.** It's faith in action, declaring God's promises and positioning yourself for breakthrough.

Jesus Himself showed the power of persistent prayer during His own struggles (**Luke 22:39-46**). He knew how important it was to stay close to the Father.

Common Prayer Challenges in Spiritual Warfare

Let's be honest; prayer can be challenging, especially in warfare. You might feel:

- **Discouraged**: Praying but not seeing immediate results
- **Distracted**: Mind wandering or wrestling with doubts
- **Tired**: Feeling spiritually drained or overwhelmed
- **Uncertain**: Not knowing what to pray or how to pray effectively

If you relate, you're not alone. These challenges are normal, but God's Word offers solutions to overcome them.

Key Prayer Strategies to Win Your Battles

1. Pray in the Spirit (Ephesians 6:18)

Praying in the Spirit means letting the Holy Spirit lead your prayers. Sometimes you use words, and other times the Spirit helps you pray in a way that goes beyond what you can say (**Romans 8:26**). When you pray like this, you're connecting with God's will, even when you don't fully understand it.

How to practice:

- Set aside quiet time to listen for the Spirit's guidance.
- Begin with simple prayers and ask the Spirit to lead you into deeper prayer.
- Use a journal to write down any thoughts or words you feel the Spirit gives you.

2. Use Scripture as Your Prayer Foundation

Praying God's Word is powerful because you are praying promises He has already spoken. Scripture is a sword (Ephesians 6:17) and praying it cuts through lies and enemy tactics.

Example:

- If you feel fear, pray **2 Timothy 1:7**: "For God has not given us a spirit of fear, but of power, love, and a sound mind."
- When facing oppression, declare **Psalm 34:17**: "The righteous cry out, and the Lord hears them; He delivers them from all their troubles."

3. Declare Authority in Jesus' Name

Jesus gave you authority over darkness. Saying "in Jesus' name" isn't just a phrase—it's a powerful declaration that you stand in His authority and power (**John 14:13-14**).

Example:

"I bind every spirit of fear, confusion, and oppression in Jesus' name. I release peace, clarity, and freedom by the power of Jesus."

4. Pray with Expectation and Persistence

God honors persistence in prayer. The parable of the persistent widow (**Luke 18:1-8**) shows us that constant, faithful prayer moves God's heart and shakes the spiritual realm.

Tip:

Don't give up if you don't see immediate results. Keep praying, trusting God is working behind the scenes.

5. Pray with Worship

Worship and prayer go hand in hand. Worship shifts your focus from the problem to the Power behind the problem; God Himself. It invites His presence and breaks the enemy's hold.

Try this:

Just like David did in the Psalms, begin your prayer with praise. Start by declaring who God is; His power, goodness, and faithfulness. Let worship and gratitude lead the way before you bring your needs or battles to Him.

Real-Life Story: Stephen's Breakthrough Through Prayer

Stephen was overwhelmed by a spiritual attack that affected his peace and family life. He felt stuck, discouraged, and unsure how to fight.

One night, Stephen committed to pray for 15 minutes every day, using Scripture to declare God's promises. He prayed in the Spirit, letting the Holy Spirit guide his words. He also praised God even when he didn't feel like it.

Little by little, things started to change. His anxiety eased, tensions at home calmed down, and a quiet peace settled in; something he hadn't felt in a long time. Stephen's story reminds us: consistent, Spirit-led prayer works, even when it feels hard.

Frequently Asked Questions About Prayer in Warfare

"What if I don't know what to say?"
Start with simple prayers like, "Help me, Lord," "Show me Your truth," or pray Scripture out loud. Ask the Holy Spirit to guide you.

"How long should I pray?"
Quality over quantity. Even short, focused prayers can be powerful. Consistency matters more than duration.

"Can I pray out loud if I'm alone?"
Absolutely! Speaking out loud helps your faith engage fully. Don't worry about how it sounds.

Reflection: How's Your Prayer Life?
- Do you pray daily?
- Do you include Scripture and worship in your prayers?
- How do you handle distractions or doubts while praying?
- Are you open to the Holy Spirit leading your prayers?
- What's one change you can make to strengthen your prayer life starting today?

Activation Prayer: "Empower My Prayer Life"

Father,

Thank You for the gift of prayer; the way I can connect with You and access Your power. Help me to pray with faith, boldness, and persistence. Teach me to pray in the Spirit, guided by Your Holy Spirit, and to use Your Word as my foundation. Give me the courage to declare my authority in Jesus' name and the patience to keep praying until I see Your victory. Fill my heart with worship and gratitude so that my prayers are pleasing to You.

In Jesus' powerful name,

Amen.

Action Step: Build Your Prayer Toolkit

This week, try these steps to strengthen your prayer life in warfare:

- Choose 3 Scriptures that address your current battles. Write them down and pray them daily.
- Set a timer for 5–10 minutes to pray in the Spirit. Listen and follow where the Spirit leads.
- Start your prayer time with a worship song or a simple praise declaration.
- Write down anything that stood out; something you felt, a thought that gave you peace, or a small answer to prayer. **Don't overthink it.**

Final Encouragement

Prayer is your most effective weapon in spiritual warfare. It connects you to God's power, shifts the atmosphere, and advances His kingdom. Don't be discouraged if it feels tough at times. God is faithful and hears every cry.

Keep praying, keep pressing in, and watch how God moves in your life and battles. Your breakthrough is on the way.

Chapter 8
Fasting and Spiritual Strength

Scripture Focus: Matthew 4:1-4

"Jesus was led by the Spirit into the wilderness to be tempted by the devil. After fasting forty days and forty nights, he was hungry. The tempter came to him and said, 'If you are the Son of God, tell these stones to become bread.' Jesus answered, 'It is written: Man shall not live on bread alone, but on every word that comes from the mouth of God.'"

Let's dive into fasting: a powerful spiritual discipline that often gets misunderstood but holds real power in spiritual warfare.

Why Fasting?

Fasting is more than just skipping meals. It's a spiritual practice that helps you grow closer to God, sharpen your spiritual senses, and strengthens your fight against the enemy.

When you fast, you're saying to God and to your spirit: "I'm serious about this battle. I'm ready to deny myself and tap into Your power."

Jesus showed us the importance of fasting before facing one of the most intense spiritual confrontations of His life; the temptation in the wilderness.

What Is Fasting?

Simply put, fasting is voluntarily giving something up; most often food, to draw closer to God. While people today may also fast from things that distract the soul, like constant noise, comfort, or self-reliance, Jesus chose to go without food. Why? Because fasting isn't just about what you give up; it's about creating space for God to fill.

It's a way to:

- **Draw closer to God** by removing distractions.
- **Increase spiritual sensitivity:** your spirit tunes in more clearly when your body isn't demanding constant attention.
- **Demonstrate dependence** on God alone for strength, not on earthly things.
- **Break strongholds and release breakthroughs:** fasting intensifies your prayers and spiritual authority.

Examples of Fasting

- **Complete Fast:** No food or drink for a specific period. (Typically short-term, like 24-36 hours)
- **Partial Fast:** Abstaining from certain types of food (like Daniel's fast of only fruits and vegetables).
- **Juice or Liquid Fast:** Only consuming liquids like water, juice, or broth.
- **Corporate Fast:** A group or church fasting together for a shared purpose.

Choose a fast that fits your health and spiritual goals. If you have medical conditions, consult a doctor first.

Biblical Examples of Fasting in Warfare

Jesus' 40-Day Fast (**Matthew 4**): Preparing for the ultimate battle with the enemy, Jesus fasted to strengthen His spirit and resist temptation.

Esther's Fast (**Esther 4:16**): Esther called for a fast before approaching the king to save her people, showing fasting's power in spiritual intercession and breakthrough.

Paul and Barnabas' Fast (**Acts 13:2-3**): Before launching their mission, they fasted and prayed, seeking God's direction and empowerment.

How Fasting Strengthens You Spiritually

1. Increases Your Spiritual Awareness

Fasting clears the noise and sharpens your spiritual senses, helping you hear God clearly and spot the enemy's tactics. When you set aside physical cravings, your spirit grows more alert and focused on God's voice.

2. Enhances Your Prayer Life

Fasting and prayer work best together. As you fast, your prayers grow stronger, helping you develop perseverance and clarity in your conversations with God.

3. Weakens the Enemy's Hold

When you fast with faith and purpose, you weaken the enemy's hold over areas of your life like anxiety, unhealthy habits, or negative thoughts. Fasting breaks strongholds by denying the enemy access to your flesh's weaknesses, giving your spirit more strength to fight back.

4. Builds Spiritual Discipline

Fasting helps you build self-control, which is a big part of spiritual warfare. When your body learns to follow God's Spirit, it makes you stronger inside and out.

Real-Life Story: Bobby's Breakthrough Through Fasting

Bobby grew up missing his dad's presence. That absence left a quiet sadness inside him, making it hard to believe he was truly loved or valued. He tried praying, going to church, and talking to counselors, but the pain still lingered.

One day, Bobby decided to fast for three days, giving up food to focus only on God. The first day was challenging; his body felt weak, and his thoughts were all over the place.

But by the second day, a calm started to fill his heart, something peaceful he hadn't known before.

By the end of the fast, Bobby found the courage to have a heart-to-heart talk with his father. That conversation helped clear the distance between them and set them both free.

More than just healing his relationship with his dad, the fast drew Bobby closer to God. It changed how he saw himself and gave him new strength and hope to face whatever came next.

How to Fast Effectively in Spiritual Warfare

1. Set Your Purpose

Decide what you're fasting for. Is it clarity, breakthrough, deliverance, or a special request? Having a clear goal focuses your spirit and prayers.

2. Prepare Spiritually and Physically

Prepare your heart by confessing sin, asking for God's strength, and committing to seek Him fully. Physically, ease into your fast by eating lighter meals beforehand.

3. Pair Fasting With Prayer and Scripture

Fasting is not just about abstaining; it's about filling up on God. Read Scripture, pray intentionally, and listen for God's voice.

4. Stay Hydrated

Drink plenty of water unless you're on a very short fast. Your body still needs hydration to function well.

5. Break Your Fast Wisely

When you end your fast, start with light, healthy foods to ease your system back in. Avoid overeating or junk food.

Common Questions About Fasting

"Is fasting required for all believers?"

No, but it's a powerful invitation from God. Fasting isn't a rule; it's a way to draw closer to Him, grow in spiritual strength, and hear His voice more clearly. It's personal, and it should be approached with wisdom and a willing heart.

"What if I fail or break my fast early?"

Don't give up. Every effort counts, and God honors your heart's intent.

"Can I fast if I have health issues?"

Consult your doctor. There are different fast types that may be safer, like partial or juice fasts.

Reflection: Is God Calling You to Fast?

- Have you ever fasted before?
- What might God want to say to you during a fast?
- What would be your purpose for fasting?
- How can you prepare your heart and body for a fast?

Activation Prayer: "Strengthen Me Through Fasting"

Lord,

I come before You ready to humble myself and seek Your face more earnestly. Help me to fast with a heart fully surrendered to You. Strengthen me when my body is weak and my mind is tempted to quit. Help me hear Your voice clearly and receive Your breakthrough. Teach me discipline and deepen my dependence on You alone. May my fasting draw me closer to You and empower me to stand strong in the battles I face.

In Jesus' name,

Amen.

Action Step: Plan Your First or Next Fast

- Choose a fast type and duration that fits your health and lifestyle.
- Set a spiritual purpose and write it down.
- Prepare with prayer and Scripture.
- Invite a trusted friend or prayer partner for accountability.
- Reflect on the experience and journal what God reveals.

Final Encouragement

Fasting is a powerful way to grow spiritually and engage in real spiritual warfare. It's not about rules or proving anything to God; it's about humbling yourself, drawing near to Him, and relying fully on His power to fight battles you can't win on your own.

Step into fasting with faith, and watch how God moves mountains on your behalf.

Chapter 9
Worship as a Weapon

Scripture Focus: 2 Chronicles 20:21-22
"After consulting the people, Jehoshaphat appointed men to sing to the Lord and to praise Him for the splendor of His holiness as they went out at the head of the army... As they began to sing and praise, the Lord set ambushes against the men of Ammon and Moab and Mount Seir who were invading Judah, and they were defeated."

Why Worship?

When people think of worship, they picture singing songs on Sunday morning or maybe private times of praise. But worship is so much more than music. Worship is a powerful weapon in spiritual warfare. It shifts atmospheres, breaks chains, and invites God's presence in ways that nothing else can.

Worship isn't just an expression; it's a declaration. It's telling the enemy, "I trust God more than my circumstances." It's an act of faith that shakes the unseen realms.

What Does It Mean to Worship?

To worship means to honor, adore, and magnify God for who He is. It's a heart posture that acknowledges God's power, goodness, and sovereignty, even in the middle of the fight.

Worship can be:

- Singing praises
- Speaking God's truths aloud
- Meditating on His character
- Giving thanks in hard times
- Living in obedience as an act of worship

Biblical Story: Jehoshaphat's Battle

One of the most vivid examples of worship as a weapon is found in **2 Chronicles 20**. King Jehoshaphat faced an overwhelming enemy alliance ready to attack Judah.

Instead of sending soldiers out first, Jehoshaphat declared a fast and sought God. Then, he appointed singers to lead the army in worship and praise as they went into battle.

As soon as the worship began, God fought for them. The enemies turned on each other and were defeated without Judah having to lift a sword.

The worship didn't just lift their spirits, it shifted the battle.

Worship Breaks Chains and Shifts Atmospheres

1. Worship Invites God's Presence

The enemy hates God's presence because it exposes darkness and releases light and power. Worship draws God close and forces the enemy to flee.

2. Worship Confuses the Enemy

Satan and his forces are shaken when believers choose worship over fear. The enemy expects us to panic or give up, but worship disrupts his plans.

3. Worship Strengthens You

When you worship, your spirit rises above the struggle. Your focus shifts from problems to the Provider. This renewed strength helps you persevere.

Real-Life Example: Paul and Silas in Prison (Acts 16:25–26)

Paul and Silas had been beaten and thrown into a dark prison cell; chained, bruised, and in pain. But instead of giving in to fear or discouragement, they did something unexpected: **they worshiped**. Around midnight, they started praying and singing songs to God.

Their worship wasn't based on how they felt. It was based on who God is.

And something amazing happened. Suddenly, **a violent earthquake shook the prison,** the doors flew open, and everyone's chains fell off. Their worship didn't just lift their spirits, it **changed the atmosphcrc** and set people free.

That's the power of worship in spiritual warfare. When you praise God, even in pain, heaven responds. Walls shake. Chains break. Freedom comes.

How to Use Worship as a Weapon

1. Make Worship a Daily Habit

Don't wait for a challenge to worship. Make worship a part of your everyday life; morning, noon, and night.

2. Sing, Speak, and Declare God's Truth

Whether you're alone or with others, speak your praise out loud. Your words have power and can tear down the enemy's tricks.

3. Use Scripture-Based Worship

Focus on who God is: His faithfulness, power, love, and victory. This roots your worship in truth.

4. Combine Worship with Prayer and Praise

Worship opens the door to deeper prayer. When you praise God, it prepares your heart to listen and pray with more power.

5. Create a Worship Space

Set aside a physical or mental place to worship regularly, even if it's just a corner of your room or a quiet moment in nature.

Common Questions About Worship

"What if I don't feel like worshiping?"

Worship isn't about feelings; it's a choice. Even when you don't feel it, choosing to worship invites God's presence and power.

"Can worship really change my circumstances?"

Yes! Worship shifts spiritual dynamics. The battle isn't always about changing circumstances immediately but changing your heart and the spiritual atmosphere.

"Is worship only singing?"

No. Worship can be expressed through your lifestyle, obedience, meditation, and gratitude.

Reflection: How Can You Make Worship Your Weapon?

- What does worship look like in your daily life?
- How can you start worshiping even when life is hard?
- What songs, scriptures, or declarations strengthen your faith?
- How might worship open doors for breakthrough in your struggles?

Activation Prayer: "Teach Me to Worship You in Spirit and Truth"

Father,

Help me to worship You; not just with my lips, but with my heart and spirit. Teach me to praise You even when I don't understand my struggles. Let worship be my weapon, breaking chains and inviting Your power. May my heart choose You above fear, doubt, and discouragement. Fill me with joy and strength as I magnify Your name every day.

In Jesus' name,

Amen.

Action Step: Worship Daily, Warfare Always

- Create a playlist of worship songs that encourage you.
- Set a daily time to worship aloud or silently.
- Memorize and declare Scriptures about God's power and victory.
- Share your worship experience with a friend or small group.

Final Encouragement

Worship isn't just something you do on Sunday, or only when everything feels perfect. It's an honor and a lifeline, a way of living that activates kingdom power every day. When you worship right in the middle of your struggles and fights, you invite heaven to break through and make way for victory.

So next time you're facing a battle, don't hold back; sing, shout, or even whisper your praise. Worship is a powerful weapon that pushes back darkness and changes everything.

Chapter 10
Deliverance and Freedom

Scripture Focus: Luke 4:18
"He has sent me to proclaim freedom for the prisoners and recovery of sight for the blind, to set the oppressed free."

What Is Deliverance?

When we talk about deliverance, many images come to mind: casting out demons, breaking chains, and freedom from bondage. Deliverance is God's powerful act of rescuing you from anything that enslaves or oppresses your mind, body, or spirit.

It's more than just a one-time event. Deliverance is a journey toward freedom: freedom from fear, addiction, depression, toxic patterns, and spiritual attacks. It's about stepping into the abundant life Jesus promised.

Why Deliverance Matters

Imagine living in a prison with invisible walls. You know freedom exists, but you can't reach it because of chains you don't fully understand. Deliverance is about breaking those chains and walking into the light.

For many, deliverance reveals areas of life where the enemy has a stronghold; sometimes from past trauma, generational curses, or spiritual oppression.

Jesus came to set the captives free, and that includes you. No matter what you face, freedom is your birthright.

Biblical Story: Jesus and the Demon-Possessed Man (Mark 5:1-20)

One of the most powerful stories of deliverance is Jesus meeting the man possessed by many demons in the region of the Gerasenes.

This man was isolated, tormented, and bound by chains. No one could help him. When Jesus arrived, He didn't negotiate or tiptoe around the enemy; He commanded the unclean spirits to leave.

The demons pleaded to be sent into a herd of pigs, which then rushed into the sea and drowned. The man was set free, fully restored, and returned to his community in peace.

This story reminds us that no situation is too dark or difficult for Jesus to rescue.

Deliverance Is for Everyone

Deliverance is not just for dramatic cases. Sometimes the enemy's hold is subtle, like anxiety, recurring sin, or toxic relationships.

Freedom might mean breaking free from bitterness, unhealthy habits, or spiritual blindness. It might mean walking away from what's familiar but harmful.

God wants you to experience real freedom, not just a taste of it, but the kind that fills every part of your life. Whether you've been walking with Him for years or you're still figuring things out, His heart is for you to live fully free.

How Does Deliverance Work?

1. Recognize the Need

The first step is awareness. Sometimes we don't realize we're in bondage because the chains have been hidden for so long.

Ask God to reveal any areas where you need healing or freedom.

2. Confess and Repent

Deliverance begins with repentance; turning away from anything that gives the enemy a foothold.

This is not about shame but about honesty and surrender.

3. Claim Jesus' Authority

Remember, Jesus has all authority (Matthew 28:18). When you speak in His name, darkness must flee.

4. Seek Prayer and Support

Sometimes deliverance happens in community, through prayer ministry, pastoral care, or trusted friends. Don't try to fight alone.

5. Walk in Freedom Daily

Deliverance is a process. Keep renewing your mind with God's Word, guard your heart, and live in obedience.

Real-Life Story: Tasha's Journey to Freedom

Tasha battled anxiety and fear throughout her young adult life. She tried everything she knew; therapy, medication, and even positive affirmations from books recommended by friends, family, and her church community. Some things helped for a little while, but the fear always crept back in.

Everything shifted when she had a personal encounter with Jesus; one she can only describe as life-changing. It wasn't just an emotional high; it was like something clicked deep in her soul. Much like Paul on the road to Damascus, her eyes were opened. She realized the battle wasn't just emotional or mental, it was spiritual.

Through prayer and support from a deliverance ministry, she began to face what was really going on beneath the surface: lies she had believed, wounds that had never healed, and spiritual strongholds that needed to be broken.

It didn't happen overnight. There were still hard moments. But step by step, peace began to replace the panic. Joy started growing where fear once lived. Tasha didn't just learn to cope, she began to walk in real freedom.

Now, she shares her story to remind others that lasting healing and freedom come not from formulas or self-help books, but through a life-changing encounter with Jesus, and by surrendering to Him as He does the deep, healing work only He can do.

Common Questions About Deliverance

"Do I have to be 'possessed' to need deliverance?"

No. Deliverance is about freedom; freedom from anything that keeps you bound, whether it's spiritual, emotional, or mental. It's not just about possession; it's about restoration. God wants to heal the whole person; breaking chains of fear, shame, bitterness, addiction, or anything else that holds you back from living in His fullness.

"It is for freedom that Christ has set us free. Stand firm, then, and do not let yourselves be burdened again by a yoke of slavery." —Galatians 5:1 (NIV)

"Is deliverance scary?"

It can be intimidating, but God's love and power overshadow fear. With the right guidance, deliverance is a safe and healing process.

"Can I do deliverance myself?"

You can pray for freedom in Jesus' name, but it's often helpful to seek pastoral or ministry support for deeper issues.

Reflection: Are You Living in Freedom?

- Are there areas in your life where you feel stuck or oppressed?
- Have you acknowledged these areas before God?
- What steps can you take to move toward freedom?
- Who can support you in this journey?

Activation Prayer: "Jesus, Set Me Free"

Lord Jesus,

Thank You for the freedom You bring into my life. I confess the areas where I've felt trapped; whether by fear, sin, or darkness. I repent and turn my heart to You. I claim Your name, knowing that at Your name every chain breaks and every enemy must flee. I ask You now to break every stronghold in my life and bring healing to my mind, body, and spirit. Fill me with Your peace and power so I can walk boldly in the freedom You give. Help me live as a victor, no longer captive but free.

In Your mighty name,

Amen.

Action Step: Take Your Next Step Toward Freedom

- Identify one area where you sense you need deliverance.
- Find a trusted pastor or ministry to pray with you.
- Begin memorizing Scripture verses about freedom and victory.
- Journal your journey, what changes do you see over time?

Final Encouragement

Deliverance isn't just some distant idea, it's God's gift to you. No matter how heavy or dark things feel right now, Jesus' light can break through all of it. I want to encourage you to step into that light and start living the freedom you were created for.

Freedom isn't something far off or out of reach. It's real, and it's waiting for you. You don't have to carry those chains any longer.

Chapter 11
Living Out Your Authority: Partnering with Jesus to Do Greater Things

Scripture Focus: John 14:12
"Very truly I tell you, whoever believes in me will do the works I have been doing, and they will do even greater things than these, because I am going to the Father."

What Does It Mean to Walk in Authority?

Walking in authority isn't just about spiritual power or standing against the enemy. It's about living every day as Jesus did; empowered by the Holy Spirit to love, serve, heal, and bring hope into the world. Jesus calls you to partner with Him to do greater things, not by your own strength, but through His Spirit working in and through you.

Authority is about stepping into your God-given role to influence your environment for good, carrying out His will in your community, workplace, and relationships. It's about making a real difference by letting God's power flow through your life.

How Authority Empowers Your Life

When you walk in authority with Jesus:

- **You step boldly into challenges** at work, school, or home with confidence.
- **You share God's love and truth** naturally, impacting those around you.
- **You become an agent of healing and hope** in places where pain and struggle exist.
- **You stand firm in faith** when facing uncertainty, knowing God is with you.
- **You live out your purpose,** doing the good works God prepared for you.

Practical Steps to Live in Authority Daily

1. Remain Connected to Jesus
Spend time daily in His Word and in prayer. Your authority flows from your relationship with Him. The more you abide in Jesus, the more His power will flow through you.

2. Listen to the Holy Spirit
Authority is led by the Spirit, not by human effort or willpower alone. Ask God to help you recognize His voice and guidance.

3. Act in Faith
Don't wait for perfect conditions. Step out when God prompts you; even if it feels uncertain or risky. Faith grows as you obey.

4. Serve Others
Use your authority to bless, encourage, and build up those around you. Authority is never about control but about loving leadership.

5. Walk Humbly
True authority comes with humility and a heart aligned with God's will. Remember, you're a servant first.

Real-Life Story: Anna's Step of Faith

Anna was nervous about sharing her faith at college. She worried she wasn't bold enough or didn't know what to say. But remembering Jesus' promise in **John 14:12**, she prayed for courage to step out. One afternoon, she noticed a friend struggling with stress and simply offered a kind word of encouragement and prayer.

That small moment opened the door for deeper conversations and a new friendship centered on faith. Anna realized authority isn't about having all the answers, it's about trusting God to work through you when you step out in love.

Reflection Questions

- How can I partner with Jesus in my daily life to do greater things?
- Where is God calling me to step out in faith right now?
- Am I listening to the Holy Spirit's guidance throughout my day?
- How can I serve others with the authority Jesus has given me?

Activation Prayer: Empower Me to Do Your Work, Jesus

Jesus,

Thank You for inviting me to do Your works and even greater things. Help me to live in Your authority by relying fully on Your Spirit, walking humbly, and loving boldly. Teach me to serve others well and trust You every step of the way. May my life reflect Your power, grace, and love, bringing hope and healing where it's needed most.

In Your powerful name,

Amen.

Action Step

This week, identify one "greater thing" God is asking you to do; whether it's a kind word, a step of faith, or an act of service, and pray for His power to accomplish it. Step out confidently, knowing you walk in the authority Jesus has given you.

Chapter 12
Spiritual Disciplines for Warfare

Scripture Focus: 1 Timothy 4:7-8
"Train yourself to be godly. For physical training is of some value, but godliness has value for all things, holding promise for both the present life and the life to come."

Why Spiritual Disciplines Matter in Spiritual Warfare

Spiritual warfare isn't just about dramatic battles or fiery prayers. It's a daily walk, a lifestyle. And just like an athlete trains consistently to win, a believer trains through spiritual disciplines to stay strong, focused, and victorious.

Spiritual disciplines are the habits and practices that shape your heart, mind, and spirit to align with God's will. They build endurance for the battles ahead and keep you growing in faith and power.

The Power of Consistency

Ever notice how small daily habits create big results? Drinking water, exercising, or practicing a skill. Over time, these add up.

The same goes for spiritual disciplines. Doing them consistently builds spiritual muscle, sharpens your senses, and deepens your intimacy with God.

Key Spiritual Disciplines for Warfare

1. Prayer

Prayer is your direct line to God. It's how you communicate, strategize, and receive power.

- **Consistent prayer** fuels your authority.
- **Intercessory prayer** fights battles for others.
- **Prayers of praise and thanksgiving** shift your atmosphere toward victory.

2. Fasting

Fasting is voluntarily giving up food or other comforts to focus on God.

- It sharpens spiritual sensitivity.
- It breaks strongholds (see Chapter 8).
- It increases power in prayer.

Jesus fasted before starting His public ministry; showing fasting's importance in spiritual preparation.

3. Bible Study and Meditation

Knowing God's Word is essential for discernment and defense.

- The Word is your sword (Ephesians 6:17).
- Meditation on Scripture fills your mind with truth, replacing lies and fear.
- The Word guides your actions in battle.

4. Worship

Worship shifts your heart and atmosphere.

- It breaks chains and binds strongholds.
- It invites God's presence, driving out darkness.
- Worship is a weapon (see Chapter 9).

5. Confession and Repentance

- Unconfessed sin weakens your defense.
- Repentance restores your connection to God.
- Confession brings healing and breaks enemy strongholds.

6. Fellowship

Spiritual warfare isn't solo.

- Being connected with other believers provides encouragement, accountability, and support.
- United prayer and worship multiply power.

Biblical Story: Daniel's Discipline (Daniel 6)

Daniel's life is a powerful example of how spiritual discipline plays a key role in spiritual warfare. Even when a royal decree made prayer a crime punishable by death, Daniel stayed faithful. He continued praying three times a day, seeking God's face, and living a life marked by integrity and devotion to Scripture.

His disciplined life wasn't just a routine, it was a lifestyle. Because of his daily devotion, God shut the mouths of lions and elevated Daniel to places of influence and favor, even in a hostile environment.

Daniel shows us that spiritual disciplines anchor us in God's presence and open the door for heaven to move on our behalf.

Real-Life Story: Todd's Journey of Discipline

Todd loved basketball. He played on his school team and trained hard, hoping to get noticed by scouts one day. But off the court, things felt off. His mind was always racing, and he couldn't shake a feeling of emptiness. He believed in God but felt distant, like they were on different teams.

After a mentor at church talked about spiritual discipline, Todd decided to make a shift. Just like he practiced drills and work-outs, he started building daily habits to grow closer to God. Every morning before school, he read a short Bible passage, prayed, and wrote down one thing he felt God was saying. Once a week, he gave up something he enjoyed, like snacks or video games, so he could focus more on God instead.

At first, it felt awkward, like learning a new play. But with time, Todd noticed something was changing. His thoughts were clear-er. He had more peace, even under pressure during games. And when challenges came on the court or in life, he didn't feel alone. He felt like God was right there, helping him through it.

Todd's story shows that discipline isn't just for sports. When you make space for God, He shows up. And that connection with God can lead to lasting peace, bold confidence, and clear direction; both on and off the court.

Overcoming Challenges to Discipline

Many believers want victory but find it hard to maintain spiritual disciplines.

Common struggles include:

- Feeling too busy
- Lack of motivation
- Doubt about the effectiveness
- Spiritual dryness

If this sounds like you, remember:

- Start small and build habits
- Ask God for help daily
- Find a prayer partner or group for encouragement
- Celebrate progress, not perfection

Reflection: Which Discipline Needs Your Focus?

Take a moment to reflect:

- Where am I strongest?
- Where do I struggle?
- What one discipline can I commit to growing this week?
- How can I create space in my schedule for this practice?

Activation Prayer: "Teach Me to Train in Spiritual Battle"

Father,

I want to be strong and grounded in the battle You've called me to fight. Teach me to pray without ceasing, to hunger for Your Word, and to worship You in spirit and truth. Help me to fast when You lead, confess quickly, and stay connected to the body of Christ. Train me daily to walk in Your power and presence.

In Jesus' name,

Amen.

Action Step: Build Your Discipline Routine

- Choose one spiritual discipline to focus on this week.
- Set a daily or weekly goal (e.g., 10 minutes of prayer, one fast, daily Bible verse).
- Journal any changes you notice in your spirit or circumstances.
- Connect with a friend or group to encourage one another.

Final Encouragement

Spiritual disciplines are not a checklist to earn God's favor; they are tools He lovingly provides to help you grow closer to Him and stand victorious.

Like an athlete trains for a marathon, your consistency prepares you for every spiritual battle and breakthrough.

Start where you are, stay faithful, and watch God transform your life step by step.

Chapter 13
Breaking Generational Strongholds

Scripture Focus: Exodus 20:5
"...for I, the Lord your God, am a jealous God, punishing the children for the sin of the parents to the third and fourth generation of those who hate me..."

What Are Generational Strongholds?

Generational strongholds are patterns of sin, bondage, curses, or spiritual problems that seem to run in families passed down from one generation to the next.

Maybe you've faced the same battles over and over; habits you can't shake, fear that keeps creeping in, or hurt that just won't heal. You've prayed, tried harder, even buried it for a while, but still wonder, "Why can't I break free?"

This chapter will help you understand what generational strongholds are, how they affect us, and most importantly, how you can break free once and for all.

Why Do Generational Strongholds Exist?

God's Word warns us about consequences of sin that affect multiple generations. But remember, God is also a God of mercy and restoration.

The enemy loves to use past hurts, curses, and patterns to keep us trapped, but Jesus came to set us free; completely free (**John 8:36**).

Generational strongholds can manifest as:

- Repeated family patterns of addiction or abuse
- Inherited fears or spiritual oppression
- Financial difficulties or curses
- Negative mindsets and soul ties

Biblical Story: The Curse Broken (**Numbers 14:18**)

God spoke through Moses, explaining that the consequences of sin could extend to multiple generations, but also that He shows "love to thousands" who keep His commandments.

Yet in the New Testament, through Jesus, the curse of sin was broken once and for all; giving us authority to break free from these chains.

Real-Life Story: Michael's Freedom Journey

Michael grew up in a family with a history of anger and addiction. For years, he felt trapped in the same cycles, even after becoming a believer.

Through prayer, counseling, and applying God's promises, Michael renounced the patterns he inherited. He forgave his ancestors, broke soul ties, and declared freedom over his life.

Today, Michael leads a ministry helping others break generational chains.

Steps to Break Generational Strongholds

1. Identify the Strongholds
- Pray for God's revelation about patterns affecting your family.
- Write down recurring struggles or curses.

2. Repent and Forgive
- Confess any personal sin related to these strongholds.
- Forgive family members and release resentment.

3. Renounce the Strongholds
- Verbally declare breaking of curses and lies.
- Use Scripture declarations (see action step).

4. Apply the Blood of Jesus
- Claim the power of Jesus' blood to cleanse and protect.
- Invite God's healing and restoration.

5. Replace with God's Promises
- Fill your mind and heart with truth from Scripture.
- Meditate on your new identity in Christ.

Reflection: What Strongholds Do I Need to Break?

Ask yourself:
- Are there patterns in my family or personal life that keep repeating?
- Have I forgiven those who hurt me or my ancestors?
- Am I ready to declare freedom and receive healing?

Activation Prayer: "Break Every Chain"

Lord Jesus,

I thank You for breaking every chain that has held me and my family captive. I renounce every curse, stronghold, and pattern that has passed down through generations. By Your blood, I declare freedom, healing, and new life. Help me walk in the fullness of Your victory, breaking every yoke of bondage. I forgive those who have hurt me and release every stronghold of bitterness. Thank You for restoring my soul and making me new.

In Your powerful name,

Amen.

Action Step: Declaration to Break Strongholds

Pray out loud daily this week:

"I break every generational stronghold over my life. I renounce every curse and lie passed down through my family line. I claim the blood of Jesus over me, my mind, body, and spirit. I am free, healed, and restored in Christ. I walk in the newness of life. Amen."

Final Encouragement

Generational burdens can feel heavy, but God's power to break them is greater.

You don't have to carry your family's struggles or repeat their mistakes.

Through Jesus, you have the authority to choose freedom, healing, and restoration.

Step into your God-given destiny and watch old patterns fall away, generation after generation.

Chapter 14
Walking in the Spirit

Scripture Focus: Galatians 5:16-25
"Walk by the Spirit, and you will not gratify the desires of the flesh."

What Does It Mean to Walk in the Spirit?

Walking in the Spirit isn't just a spiritual cliché, it's the heart of living a victorious, empowered Christ-like life. The Bible teaches us that there are two ways to live: by the flesh or by the Spirit. When you walk in the flesh, you're driven by self, desires, and weaknesses. But when you walk in the Spirit, you live under God's guidance, power, and peace.

Paul tells us clearly; **"Walk by the Spirit, and you will not gratify the desires of the flesh."** This means our daily choices, thoughts, and actions are influenced by the Holy Spirit working in us.

What Does Walking in the Spirit Look Like?

Walking in the Spirit means:

- Letting God's Spirit lead your decisions.
- Responding to challenges with love, joy, and peace.

- Experiencing the fruit of the Spirit in your life (love, joy, peace, patience, kindness, goodness, faithfulness, gentleness, and self-control).
- Rejecting sinful patterns and choosing obedience.
- Hearing God's voice and obeying His prompting.

Biblical Story: Peter's Transformation

Peter, one of Jesus' closest followers, often acted impulsively in the flesh. He denied Jesus three times out of fear and confusion (**Luke 22:54-62**). But after Pentecost, filled with the Holy Spirit, Peter boldly preached, healed, and stood firm in faith (**Acts 2**).

What changed? Walking in the Spirit transformed his heart and empowered his actions. You, too, can experience this kind of transformation by walking in the Spirit daily.

Real-Life Story: Paul's Journey from Fear to Faith

Paul had been feeling God's call to leave his job for years. He sensed a deep pull toward ministry, especially leading youth, but fear held him back. Questions swirled in his mind: *What about the bills? How will I provide? Is this really the right step?*

The uncertainty kept him stuck, caught between the comfort of a paycheck and the risk of stepping into the unknown. But Paul decided to stop wrestling alone and began praying daily for the Holy Spirit's guidance, courage, and peace.

Slowly, God started changing Paul's heart. Instead of fear, he began to feel boldness and clarity. He started taking small steps; volunteering with youth groups, sharing his faith, and trusting God for provision. The fruit of the Spirit: faith, patience, and love grew stronger, helping Paul move forward.

Paul's journey wasn't quick or easy, but by leaning on God each day, he transitioned from fear to faith, stepping confidently into the ministry God had prepared for him.

1. Start with a Heart Check

Begin your day asking: Lord, what do You want to do through me today? Invite the Spirit to lead your steps and words.

2. Stay Connected to God's Word

The Spirit uses Scripture to guide and correct you. Meditate on verses about the Spirit and your identity in Christ.

3. Practice Listening

Quiet yourself and listen for the Spirit's promptings. It might come as a thought, a peace in your heart, or a sudden idea.

4. Choose Obedience

Walking in the Spirit means acting on what you hear. It's a daily choice to obey, even when it's hard.

5. Reject Fleshly Desires

Recognize patterns that lead you away from God: anger, envy, impatience, and consciously say no.

Reflection: How Spirit-Led Is My Life?

Ask yourself:

- Am I sensitive to the Spirit's leading?
- Where am I relying on my own strength instead of God's?
- How can I cultivate more of the Spirit's fruit in my daily life?

Activation Prayer: "Fill Me, Holy Spirit"

Holy Spirit,

I invite You to lead my steps and fill my heart today. Help me to walk in Your power, not my own. Teach me to love when it's hard, to be patient when I'm tired, and to choose peace over chaos. Show me the areas where I'm living by the flesh and give me strength to turn back to You. May Your fruit grow in me, so others see Jesus through my life.

In Jesus' name,

Amen.

Action Step: Daily Spirit Walk

For the next week, spend five minutes each morning asking the Holy Spirit to guide you through the day. At night, reflect on moments when you sensed His leading or missed it. Journal your experiences and growth.

Final Encouragement

Walking in the Spirit is a journey, not a perfect performance. There will be good days and hard days, but the Spirit is faithful to guide and empower you.

When you choose to walk in the Spirit, you tap into God's power for victory, peace, and transformation.

Keep stepping forward; your best days in the Spirit are ahead.

Chapter 15
Breaking Strongholds Through Prayer

Introduction:

In Chapter 13, we exposed and broke generational patterns; those inherited mindsets, behaviors, and spiritual weights that tried to shape your story. But here's the truth: freedom must be protected. The enemy doesn't give up just because you've taken a step forward. He waits, hoping you'll slip back into old cycles.

That's where prayer becomes your greatest weapon.

Breaking strongholds isn't just about identifying them, it's about tearing them down through consistent, faith-filled prayer. Strongholds lose power when you confront them with God's truth. This chapter will show you how to fight back and walk daily in victory, not just for yourself, but for the generations to come.

Scripture Focus: 2 Corinthians 10:4–5
"The weapons we fight with are not the weapons of the world. On the contrary, they have divine power to demolish strongholds."

What Are Strongholds?

Strongholds are not just physical obstacles, they're deeply rooted lies, fears, habits, and thought patterns that set themselves up against the truth of God. They hold us back, keep us stuck, and cloud our identity in Christ. You may not see them, but you feel their heaviness every time you try to move forward and hit the same wall.

They often show up as:

- A constant need for approval
- Negative self-talk or shame
- Addictive behaviors or destructive habits
- Paralyzing fear or insecurity

Biblical Story: Paul's Fight for a Free Mind

The Apostle Paul understood the battle for the mind. He faced rejection, persecution, and even physical torment, but he refused to let those experiences define him. He chose to fix his thoughts on God's truth. In prison or on the mission field, Paul prayed, praised, and preached. His example shows that strongholds don't fall through willpower; they fall through spiritual power.

Real-Life Story: Rachel's Battle with Control

Rachel always felt the need to have everything perfectly planned. She managed her life like a checklist; school, job, relationships, never leaving room for uncertainty. Deep down, though, she struggled with anxiety masked as control. The idea of surrendering anything to God felt risky. What if things fell apart?

Over time, the pressure wore her down. She couldn't sleep. Her relationships became strained. That's when Rachel finally realized her need to control everything wasn't strength. It was a stronghold.

Rachel began praying differently; not asking God to bless her plans, but asking Him to lead. Each day, she set aside time to sit in silence, read Scripture, and surrender her agenda. She even fasted from social media for a month, creating space to hear God's voice more clearly.

As she released control, peace began to grow. Her decisions weren't always easy, but they were no longer driven by fear. Rachel started trusting God, and in return, she gained clarity, rest, and deeper faith.

Her journey reminds us: strongholds don't always look like rebellion; they can show up as self-reliance. But when prayer becomes surrender, God steps in, takes the lead, and everything begins to change.

How to Identify Strongholds

Freedom begins with honesty. Ask yourself:

- What thought patterns or habits won't go away?
- Where do I feel stuck or defeated no matter how hard I try?
- What lies have I believed about myself or God?

These are often signs of a stronghold. Don't ignore them; confront them.

How Prayer Breaks Strongholds

Prayer is not passive. It's a weapon. Through prayer, you:

1. Name the stronghold. Don't generalize; call it what it is.
2. Declare God's truth. Replace every lie with Scripture.
3. Pray persistently. Strongholds don't fall in a day. Keep going.
4. Command it to fall. Pray with faith and authority in Jesus' name.

Replace the Lie with Truth

Strongholds stay alive through deception. But truth renews the mind. Here are promises to stand on:

- "God gave us a spirit not of fear but of power, love, and self-control." (**2 Timothy 1:7**)
- "I can do all things through Christ who strengthens me." (**Philippians 4:13**)
- "You will know the truth, and the truth will set you free." (**John 8:32**)

The more you meditate on truth, the more your mindset begins to shift.

Reflection: Am I Fighting Back or Giving In?

- What lies or struggles have lingered for too long?
- Am I using prayer as a weapon or a last resort?
- What truth do I need to start declaring daily?

Activation Prayer: "Tear Down Every Stronghold"

Jesus,

I come to You ready for change. I name every lie, fear, or habit that has set itself up against Your truth. I command every stronghold to fall in Your name. Fill my mind with Your peace and my heart with Your Word. I receive the power and authority You've given me. I declare: I am free, healed, and made new through You.

Amen.

Action Step: Start a Stronghold-Breaking Routine

This week, pick one stronghold. Write it down. Find two scriptures that speak against it. Pray those scriptures out loud every day for seven days.

Example: **Stronghold: Fear of failure**

Truth: "God is with me wherever I go." (**Joshua 1:9**)
Truth: "In Christ, I am more than a conqueror." (**Romans 8:37**)

Declare. Believe. Repeat.

Final Encouragement

You don't have to live at the mercy of the same battles. God's truth demolishes strongholds. His power is working in you, and prayer is your lifeline. Don't settle for survival when God has called you to walk in victory. Keep praying. Keep declaring. Keep standing. Freedom isn't just possible, it's promised.

Chapter 16
Maintaining Victory in Daily Life

Scripture Focus: 1 Corinthians 15:57
"But thanks be to God! He gives us the victory through our Lord Jesus Christ."

Victory Isn't Just a Moment: It's a Daily Choice

You know that feeling when you win a battle? It's exhilarating. But what happens after the battle? Spiritual warfare doesn't end with one victory; it's an ongoing fight. The key isn't just winning once, but **maintaining** that victory every single day.

Think of it like running a marathon, not a sprint. You don't just cross the finish line and stop; you pace yourself, hydrate, and keep moving forward.

Biblical Story: David's Daily Battle

David was called "a man after God's own heart," yet his life was full of battles; both external and internal. After defeating Goliath, David still faced many challenges: enemies, temptations, and his own mistakes. What kept David victorious wasn't just a single win but his daily reliance on God through prayer, worship, and obedience.

This shows us that maintaining victory means staying connected to God daily, no matter the ups and downs.

Real-Life Story: Sam's Consistent Walk

Sam was a believer with big plans. He worked hard, dreamed big, and thought he knew the path God wanted for him. Promotions, growing income, and promising relationships all seemed part of the plan. But deep inside, Sam wrestled with a quiet but persistent feeling. Is this really what God wants?

Like many of us, Sam wanted God to bless his plans. But over time, he realized that God often has a different plan; a better plan. The world offers success, comfort, and easy answers, but following God means sometimes saying no to those things, even when it's hard.

Sam faced choices that tested his faith. Offers promising more money but requiring compromise. Relationships that seemed right but didn't align with God's purpose. Each time, he prayed not just for God to bless his plans, but for God to lead him, even if it meant letting go of his own.

It wasn't easy. Sam wrestled with doubt and fear. But as he surrendered control, he found peace. He learned what Jesus said in **Matthew 6:33**, "But seek first the kingdom of God and his righteousness, and all these things will be added to you." And in **Proverbs 3:5-6**, "Trust in the Lord with all your heart, and do not lean on your own understanding. In all your ways acknowledge him, and he will make straight your paths."

Sam's faith grew stronger, not because life got easier, but because he trusted God's timing and purpose more than his own.

Sam's story reminds us: We may have plans, but God has the final say. Choosing to follow Him means letting go of our own agendas and trusting His guidance, even when the world's treasures call our name. When we surrender, God replaces uncertainty with peace, and His perfect plan unfolds.

Keys to Maintaining Victory

1. Stay Rooted in the Word

God's Word is your daily nourishment. It reminds you of who you are, what God has done, and how to stand strong.

2. Keep a Consistent Prayer Life

Prayer isn't just for emergencies; it's your ongoing connection to God's power. Make it a habit, not a last resort.

3. Live in Obedience

When you obey God, you protect the freedom He's given you. It might not always be easy, but obedience keeps you walking in His will.

4. Surround Yourself with Support

Community matters. Fellowship with other believers encourages you, holds you accountable, and strengthens your spiritual walk.

5. Be Watchful and Alert

The enemy never sleeps. Stay vigilant; recognize temptations and attacks early, so you can stand firm and resist.

Reflection: How Am I Maintaining My Victory?

Ask yourself:

- What daily habits keep me connected to God?
- How consistent is my prayer life?
- Who encourages and supports me spiritually?
- Am I alert to the enemy's tactics in my life?

Activation Prayer: "Help Me Stand Firm"

Father,

Thank You for the victory You've given me.
Help me maintain it every day through Your Word, prayer, and obedience. Surround me with godly friends who encourage me.
Keep me alert to the enemy's schemes. I choose to stand firm in Jesus' name, and walk in the fullness of the victory You provide.

Amen.

Action Step: Build Your Victory Toolkit

Create a simple "victory toolkit" of daily habits: Bible reading, prayer, worship, and fellowship. Write down what works best for you and commit to practicing it every day, even when you don't feel like it.

Final Encouragement

Remember, victory is a daily decision. Every moment you choose God, you claim your place as a conqueror. Don't get discouraged if you stumble. Get back up and keep pressing forward.

You've got this, because God's got you.

Chapter 17
Living as a Victor: Your New Identity

Scripture Focus: Romans 8:37
"In all these things we are more than conquerors through him who loved us."

Victory Is More Than a Moment: It's Who You Are Now

Imagine waking up every day knowing you're not just surviving; you're **winning**. Not just by chance or luck, but because you're part of something greater.

That's what it means to live as a **victor**. This isn't about boasting or pretending. It's about **owning the identity** Jesus has given you. The good news? You're not a victim. You're more than a conqueror.

Biblical Story: Paul's Unshakable Confidence

Paul faced shipwrecks, imprisonments, betrayals, and constant opposition, and yet he wrote, *"We are more than conquerors"*. His confidence wasn't from his strength but from his identity in Christ. Paul knew who he was because he knew who God was working in him.

If Paul could face all that hardship and still walk in victory, so can you.

Real-Life Story: Danielle's Journey from Fear to Freedom

Danielle had felt scared and worthless for a long time. She thought her mistakes and the things she'd done wrong meant she was stuck and could never be better. Even little things like looking in the mirror or making friends felt really hard.

Then Danielle met Jesus. At first, things didn't change all at once, but slowly she started to see that God loved her no matter what. She learned that her worth didn't come from what she did or what others said, but from God's love for her.

It was like being trapped in a prison and then someone gave her the keys to get out. Danielle realized she wasn't a prisoner of her past anymore, she was God's child. The lies she believed before didn't have power over her anymore.

Danielle says, "I used to wake up scared, worried about the day ahead. But when I understood that God loves me and has a plan for me, everything changed. Now, I live with hope instead of fear." Her freedom didn't come all at once. Some days were still tough. But every time she prayed, read the Bible, or remembered what God promised, she felt stronger and freer.

Danielle's story shows us that no matter what you've done or what you're afraid of, God's love is bigger. You can choose to believe that and start living free, one step at a time.

Your New Identity Includes:

- **Child of God**
  You're deeply loved and accepted, not because of what you've done, but because of who God says you are.

- **More Than a Conqueror**
  Life's battles don't define you; God's victory does.

- **New Creation**
  The old has gone, the new has come. Your past mistakes don't hold you back anymore.

- **Ambassador of Heaven**
  You carry God's message of hope, freedom, and love to the world around you.

- **Soldier in God's Army**
  You're part of a greater mission, equipped and empowered to stand strong.

How to Live as a Victor Daily

1. Know Your Identity

Speak it out loud. Believe it. Live it. When doubts come, remind yourself who you are in Christ.

2. Walk in Confidence

Let your actions reflect your identity. Confidence doesn't mean arrogance; it means trust in God's power working through you.

3. Resist the Enemy's Lies

The enemy will try to convince you you're defeated or unworthy. But you are victorious. Don't believe the lies.

4. Carry Hope to Others

Your victory can inspire others. Share your story and encourage those still struggling.

Reflection: Am I Living as a Victor?

Ask yourself:

- Do I truly believe I am more than a conqueror?
- How do I respond when the enemy attacks?
- Am I living from my new identity, or old labels and fears?
- How can I encourage others with my victory story?

Activation Prayer: "Help Me Live as a Victor"

Lord Jesus,

Thank You for making me more than a conqueror. Help me live every day in the confidence of my new identity. Give me boldness to resist the enemy's lies and walk in freedom. Use me to bring hope and victory to those around me. I am Yours, victorious and free.

In Your powerful name,

Amen.

Action Step: Declare Your Identity

Every morning this week, declare your new identity out loud. Speak words like:

- "I am a child of God."
- "I am more than a conqueror."
- "I am free and victorious in Jesus."

Watch how this changes your mindset and strengthens your walk.

Final Encouragement

You don't have to prove your worth or fight for acceptance. It's already yours through Jesus. Living as a victor means embracing that truth daily and stepping boldly into the life God has prepared for you.

Your identity is secure. Your victory is real. Now, live it out loud.

Conclusion

Congratulations, you've journeyed through this guide on spiritual warfare and discovered the truth: **victory isn't just a one-time event; it's a lifestyle**. It's a daily choice to stand firm, walk in authority, and live free in the power of Jesus.

Victory Is Not Occasional: It's Your New Normal

You might be thinking, ***"Spiritual battles never stop, so how can I really live in victory all the time?"*** That's a great question. Yes, the enemy will keep coming, but so will God's strength, your authority, and the freedom Jesus has already won for you.

Victory is not about never struggling. It's about never staying defeated. It's about knowing who you are in Christ; a warrior, an overcomer, and refusing to back down.

What Living in Victory Looks Like

- Boldness to face challenges without fear
- Peace that guards your heart and mind even when storms rage
- Authority to speak truth and overcome lies
- Joy and gratitude as natural responses, not occasional feelings
- Love that overflows from your relationship with God to others

Your Battle Belongs to the Lord

Remember, you don't carry this burden alone. The battle belongs to the Lord. When you stand firm in faith, the enemy must flee. When you pray, the gates of hell tremble. When you praise, darkness loses ground.

You are not powerless. You are not forgotten. You are deeply loved and fully equipped.

Encouragement for Seekers and Believers Alike

If you're reading this and you don't yet know Jesus, know this: victory is available to you too. It's not about being perfect or having it all together. It's about stepping into a relationship with the One who conquered sin and death; Jesus Christ. He invites you to join His victory team, no matter your past.

If you are a believer, be encouraged. God has already given you everything you need. Keep standing, keep fighting, keep walking boldly.

Activation Prayer: "Help Me Live in Victory Every Day"

Father,

Thank You that victory is not a distant dream but my present reality. Help me to walk each day in Your strength and authority. Remind me that You fight for me, that I am never alone. Teach me to pray with power, worship with passion, and live with boldness. Keep my eyes fixed on Jesus, my source of victory and hope.

In Your mighty name,

Amen.

Final Challenge: Live Like a Victorious Warrior

- **Keep praying:** don't give up
- **Keep praising:** celebrate every small win
- **Keep standing firm:** the enemy can't stand against God's children
- **Keep walking in faith:** even when you don't see the whole path

Victory is yours because Jesus is with you; today, tomorrow, and always. You were created to be a shining light in dark places, a fearless warrior in God's kingdom.

Live like the victor you are.

A Final Word Just for You

Hey, I want to be real with you for a second. No matter what's happened or what you're going through right now, your past doesn't have to hold you back. God's love is way bigger than any fear or mistake you might be carrying. Just like Sarah, you can start living from a place of freedom and hope; one day at a time.

This guide? It's here to help you fight the spiritual battles that try to slow you down. To show you how prayer, God's Word, and faith can be your strongest weapons when life gets tough.

It won't always be easy. Some days will still feel hard, and that's okay. But every time you choose to turn to God, to pray and hold on to His promises, you're getting stronger. You're getting closer to the life He wants for you.

You're not alone in this. God's right there with you, every step, ready to help you break free and live victorious. So keep going. Keep trusting. Keep stepping forward. Your story isn't over. The best is yet to come.

www.ingramcontent.com/pod-product-compliance
Lightning Source LLC
Chambersburg PA
CBHW051540120626
46551CB00013B/1310